IMAGES
of America

SCITUATE
RHODE ISLAND

SCITUATE
INCORPORATED
1730
NAMED FOR
SCITUATE,
MASSACHUSETTS
NAME OF
INDIAN ORIGIN

IMAGES
of America

SCITUATE
RHODE ISLAND

Heritage Room Committee

ARCADIA
PUBLISHING

Copyright © 1998 by Heritage Room Committee
ISBN 9781531641863

Published by Arcadia Publishing
Charleston, South Carolina

Library of Congress Catalog Card Number: 2008942215

For all general information contact Arcadia Publishing at:
Telephone 843-853-2070
Fax 843-853-0044
E-mail sales@arcadiapublishing.com
For customer service and orders:
Toll-Free 1-888-313-2665

Visit us on the Internet at www.arcadiapublishing.com

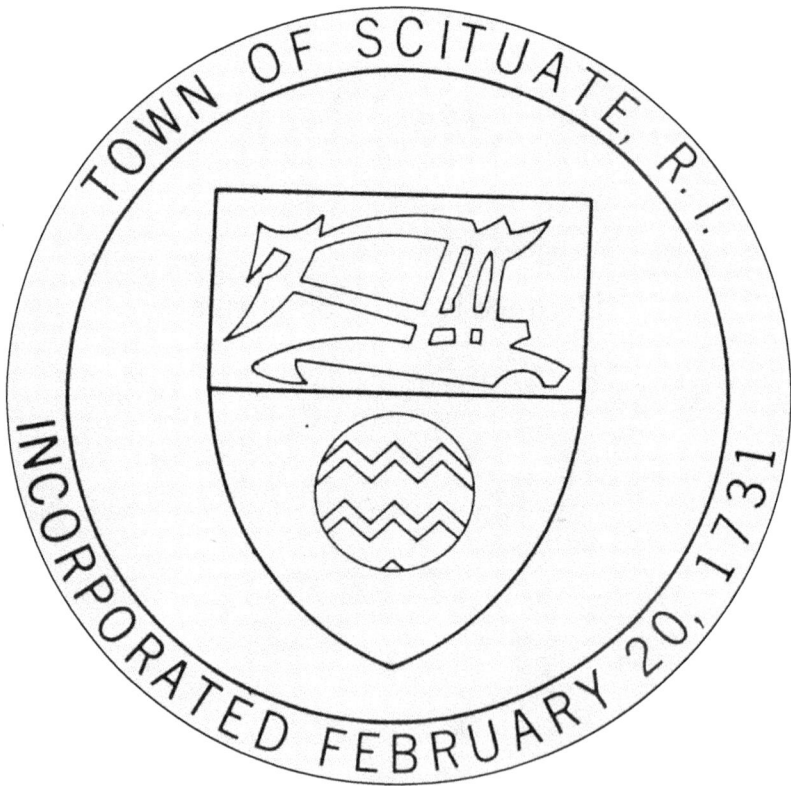

Contents

Acknowledgments

This photographic history of Scituate was drawn primarily from the large collection of materials preserved in the Heritage Room. The Heritage Room was founded in 1988 by Shirley D. Arnold, Eleanor R. Guy, and Ellen S. Pearson. Over the last ten years, the collection has grown tremendously, due to the generosity and interest of many people in Scituate history.

The book would not have been possible without the help of Barbara Sarkesian and Frank K. Spencer, Town Historians, and David Smith, photographer. We also want to acknowledge and thank the following people: Charles Atwood, Donald Carpenter, Eleanor Carpenter, Robert Dexter, the Joslin Family, Joyce Murray, Frank Searle, Herbert Walker, and the many others who responded to our request for material for this book.

Introduction

The town of Scituate is located about 10 miles west of Providence, Rhode Island. It is bordered on the north by Glocester, the east by Johnston and Cranston, the south by Coventry, and the west by Foster.

In 1638 Roger Williams received a deed for this land from the Native Americans who had settled on the shores of beautiful Moswansicut Lake. In 1662 William Vaughn and associates bought the land known as the Westconnaug Purchase and the owners drew lots for their parcels. In 1694 the first white settler, John Mathewson, laid claim to 40 acres on the northern end of the Moswansicut Lake. His first home was a hovel of logs, twigs, and mud with a hole on top to ward off the bears. By 1710 settlers from Massachusetts were claiming land, and it is said, they brought the name "Satuit," or Scituate, with them.

In 1731 the town of Scituate was incorporated and it became known for its many farms, sawmills, and gristmills. In 1765 the Brown Brothers and Stephen Hopkins purchased land in the Hope section of town on the Pawtuxet River. There they established the Hope Furnace for making iron and in 1776 it was casting cannons for the Revolutionary War effort.

It was the availability of water from the many ponds and streams that brought manufacturing to Scituate in 1806. The larger mills made cotton and woolen goods, shoe and corset laces, shoes, and combs. There were many smaller shops such as machine shops, wheelwright shops, and blacksmith shops. There was also the Nipmuc quarry, which provided Providence with a great supply of granite for its construction projects. Scituate had very rocky land which had to be cleared before the farmers could plant their crops—thus, the stone walls that are seen throughout the area.

The town of Scituate grew to include many villages, such as Ashland, Clayville, North Scituate, South Scituate, Rockland, Richmond, Hope, Jackson,

Fiskeville, Glenford, Elmdale, Kent, Harrisdale, Ponaganset, Potterville, Saundersville, and Wilbur Hollow. The abundance of water had made Scituate a booming manufacturing center in the 1800s.

In 1915 Scituate became the chosen site for a reservoir to provide much needed water to the city of Providence. The reservoir site, which encompassed 38% (or 25 sq. miles) of Scituate at the time, included over 1,000 buildings—including: 375 homes, 233 barns, 30 dairy farms, 7 schools, 6 churches, 6 large mills, plus post offices, taverns, ice houses, general stores, blacksmith shops, wheelwright shops, and many other small businesses. Several main highways had to be rerouted and new ones built. The Providence & Danielson Railway, which provided the only public transportation for people, supplies, and manufactured goods from Providence to Scituate, ceased with the coming of the reservoir.

The loss of homes and livelihoods was a traumatic experience for the many workers and families who had lived in Scituate for generations. This is the unique history of the Lost Villages of Scituate and the people who have made this history. It has been very difficult choosing the over two hundred pictures that follow from the large collection which we have worked so hard to collect and preserve in the Heritage Room. We have attempted to show you what Scituate was, and what it is today—a quiet, rural town of people working together to preserve our rich heritage.

Shirley D. Arnold
Eleanor R. Guy
Ruth S. Rounds
Heritage Room Committee

One

Homes and Farms

The Angell Homestead was located in Richmond Village on the north side of the Old Plainfield Pike, now under the Scituate Reservoir.

This home was built in 1846 by Rev. Reuben Allen, the minister of the Free Will Baptist Church. In 1918 it was owned by William E. Spencer Sr., and became known as the Granite Farm. It is located on Danielson Pike, North Scituate, and Frank K. Spencer resides here today.

The Granite Farm dairy was located across the street from the home. William E. Spencer and his sons delivered milk throughout Scituate. The barn is the site of a restaurant today.

Remington Dairy Farm, located in Hope, was founded in 1875 by the Remington family. The farm began with just six cows and soon became one of the largest dairy farms in Rhode Island.

Remington Dairy trucks were a familiar sight around the state of Rhode Island with more than 14 trucks delivering as far away as Jamestown. The Dairy Bar was added in the 1940s and the business continued until the 1960s. Their ice cream was the best in the state.

The Peckham/Budlong Farm was located on Peeptoad Road, North Scituate. The house was built about 1850 and is there today.

The Peckham/Budlong Farm was originally one of the larger local farms, producing tons of hay as its main crop.

The Poole/Barber/Round farmhouse was built in the late 1700s and was a tavern and stagecoach stop. This farm was located on Hartford Avenue, North Scituate.

The above farm was known as the Moswansicut Poultry Farm, but by the 1930s its main crop was gladiolas. It is now the site of the Scituate Shopping Center.

The Harris/Ben Smith Farm, located on both sides of West Greenville Road, was built about 1775. The farm was large, with about 200 acres of land on both sides of Pole Bridge Road and Rice's Plat. The large farmhouse remains there today.

The barns on the Harris/Ben Smith Farm housed more than 300 cows. About 15 hired hands ran the dairy and grew the hay and corn to feed the herd. The extensive stonewalls bordering the property were built about 1905.

14

This house was for the hired hands on the Harris/Ben Smith Farm. It is still located on Peeptoad Road, North Scituate, and is a private residence today.

This tea house was built by Ben Smith and was located on the beautiful west shore of the Moswansicut Lake on the farm.

This house was known as the Great House and was built by William West in 1775. It was located on the north side of Danielson Pike, about 3 miles west of the village of North Scituate.

The Potter Homestead, built in the early 1700s, is still standing on Old Plainfield Pike in Potterville. It was used as a tavern until the late nineteenth century. At the time of the Dorr Rebellion, it is said that five hundred soldiers camped here on the way to Acotes Hill in Chepachet, RI.

16

The Capt. Richard Rhodes House, now the R.I. State Police Headquarters, is located on Danielson Pike. Rhodes, a sea captain, built this house in 1794 and the farm operated for more than a century.

In 1912 the Rhodes House became the home of John W. Coggeshall and it was renovated into a luxurious mansion. It became the R.I. State Police Headquarters in 1936.

These two views are of the Joslin family home which was located in Richmond Village. The Joslins were prominent mill owners in Scituate. In 1924 they moved to their new home on Field Hill Road, Clayville.

Two

Mills

Ponaganset Mill was one of the larger mills condemned by the Providence Water Supply Board in 1915. By 1860 there were about 15 cotton mills in Scituate employing about 20% of the 4,500 people living here. The following pages show only a few of the many mills standing before the Scituate Reservoir was constructed.

NAME	FORMER OWNERS
ASHLAND MILL	ASHLAND CO.
NO. SCITUATE COTTON MILLS	NO. SCIT. COTTON MILLS
PONAGANSET RESERVOIR	PONAGANSET RES CO
BARDEN RESERVOIR	BARDEN RES CO
RICHMOND MILL	
ROCKLAND MILL	
RED MILL	JOSLIN MFG CO
UPPER CLAYVILLE MILL	
LOWER CLAYVILLE MILL	
PONAGANSET MILL	
SHODDY MILL	
REMINGTON MILL	SCITUATE LIGHT & POWER CO
SAUNDERSVILLE PRIVILEGES (UPPER, MIDDLE & LOWER)	

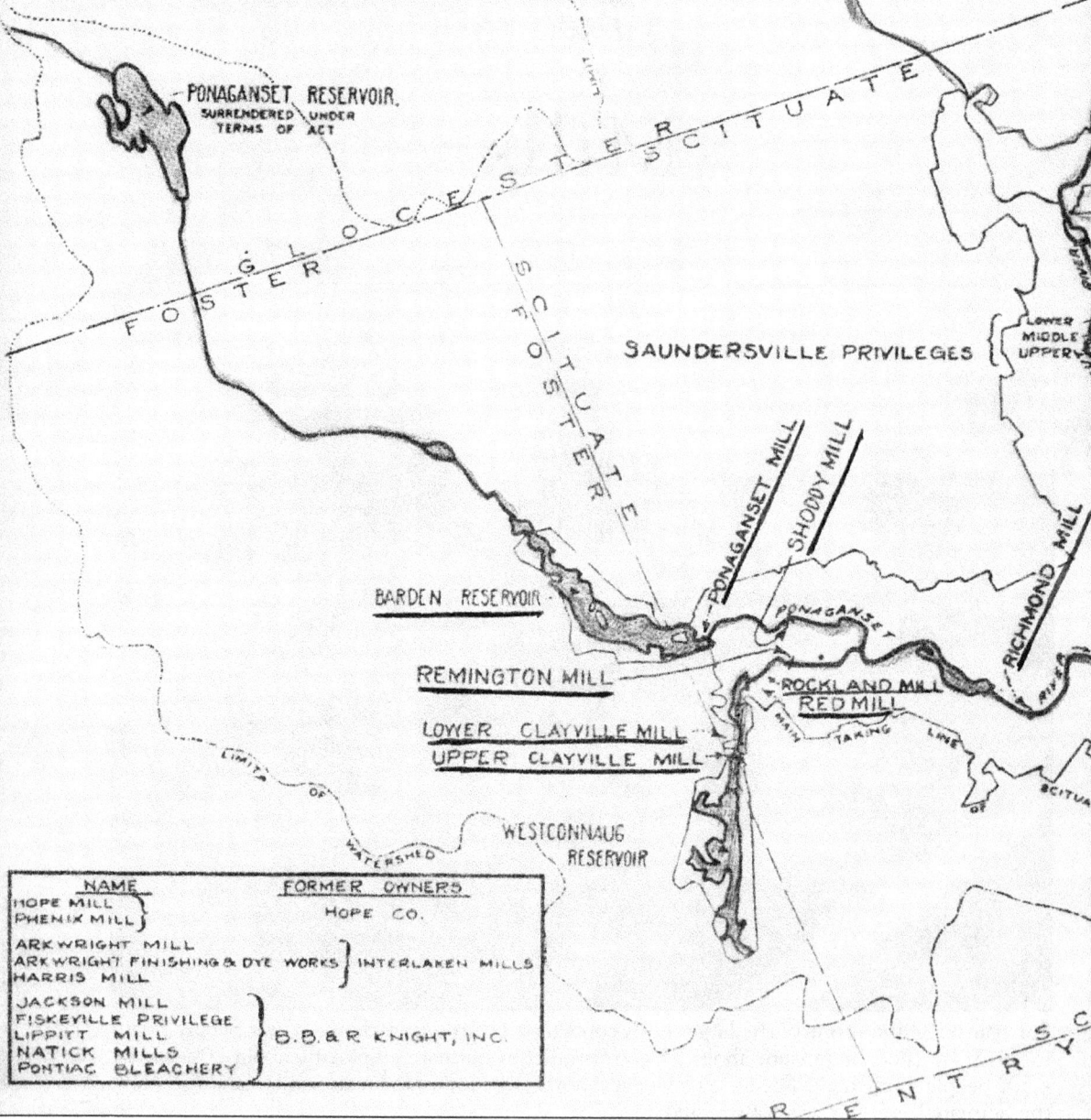

COMAN RESERVOIR

WATERSHED

PONAGANSET RESERVOIR.
SURRENDERED UNDER TERMS OF ACT

GLOCESTER SCITUATE

FOSTER

SCITUATE FOSTER

SAUNDERSVILLE PRIVILEGES

LOWER MIDDLE UPPER

RIVER

PONAGANSET MILL

SHODDY MILL

RICHMOND MILL

BARDEN RESERVOIR

PONAGANSET

REMINGTON MILL

ROCKLAND MILL
RED MILL

MAIN TAKING LINE

SCITUATE

LOWER CLAYVILLE MILL
UPPER CLAYVILLE MILL

RIVER

LIMIT OF WATERSHED

WESTCONNAUG RESERVOIR

NAME	FORMER OWNERS
HOPE MILL	HOPE CO.
PHENIX MILL	
ARKWRIGHT MILL	
ARKWRIGHT FINISHING & DYE WORKS	INTERLAKEN MILLS
HARRIS MILL	
JACKSON MILL	
FISKEVILLE PRIVILEGE	
LIPPITT MILL	B. B. & R. KNIGHT, INC.
NATICK MILLS	
PONTIAC BLEACHERY	

RENTRY SC

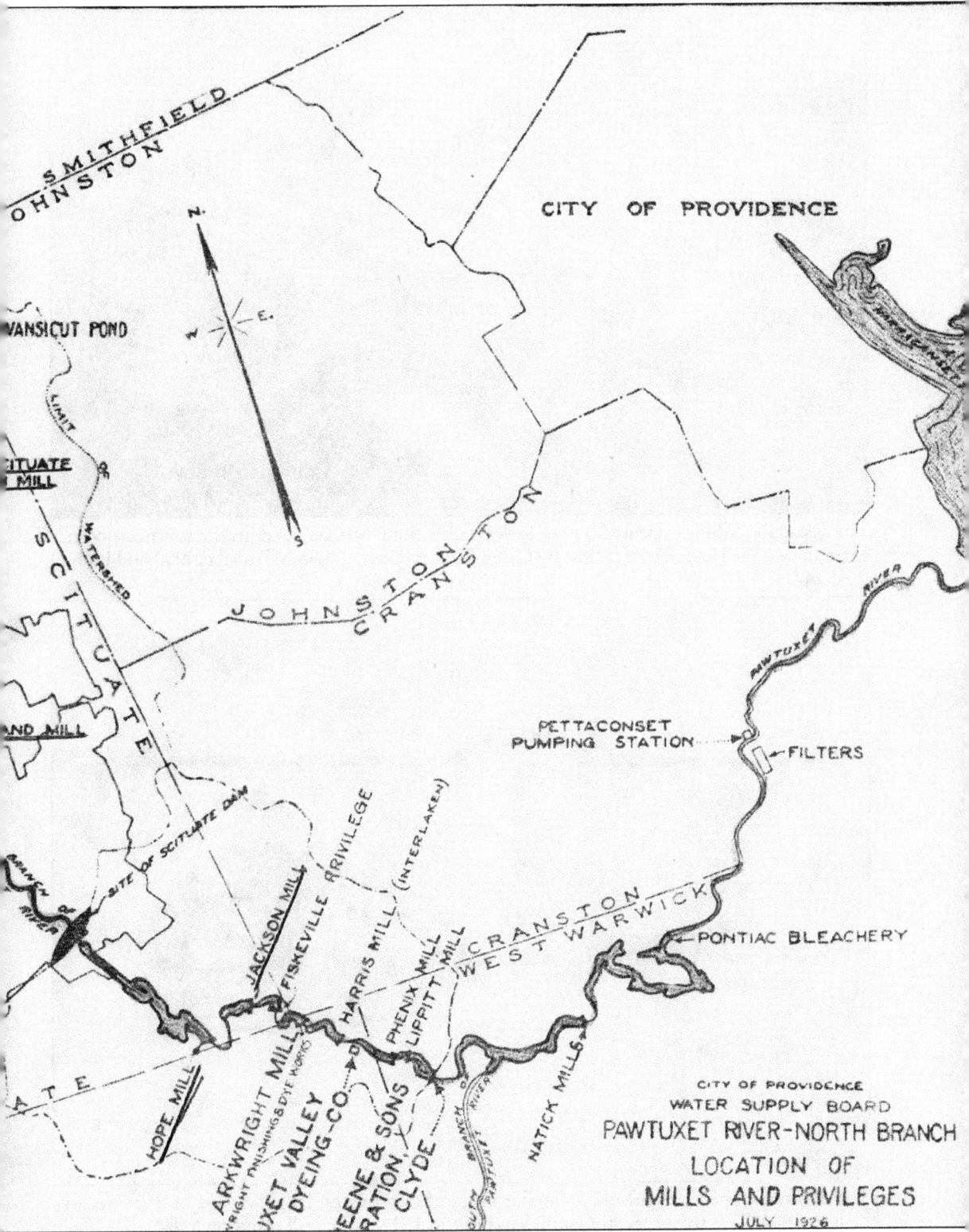

SMITHFIELD
JOHNSTON

CITY OF PROVIDENCE

N

E.

W

S

VANSICUT POND

LIMIT OF

SCITUATE
MILL

WATERSHED

SCITUATE

JOHNSTON

CRANSTON

AND MILL

PAWTUXET

RIVER

PETTACONSET
PUMPING STATION

FILTERS

BRANCH OF
RIVER

SITE OF SCITUATE DAM

JACKSON MILL

FISKEVILLE PRIVILEGE

HARRIS MILL

PHENIX MILL (INTERLAKEN)

LIPPITT MILL

CRANSTON
WEST WARWICK

PONTIAC BLEACHERY

HOPE MILL

ARKWRIGHT MILLS
WRIGHT FINISHING & DYE WORKS

XET VALLEY
DYEING CO.

EENE & SONS
RATION,
CLYDE

SOUTH BRANCH OF
PAWTUXET RIVER

NATICK MILLS

ATE

CITY OF PROVIDENCE
WATER SUPPLY BOARD
PAWTUXET RIVER-NORTH BRANCH
LOCATION OF
MILLS AND PRIVILEGES
JULY 1926

21

The Fiskeville Mill was located on the lower end of the Pawtuxet River in the southeast corner of Scituate near Hope. Built *c.* 1814 by Caleb Fiske & Son, it operated until *c.* 1900 and burned in 1914.

The original Hope Cotton Mill, located on Main Street in the Hope Village of Scituate, was built in 1806. This five-story stone mill was built in 1844 and is still standing today.

The Lower and Upper Clayville Mills were located in the village of Clayville. They were built about 1857 on the Westconnaug River. The mills manufactured combs, rubber shoes, and cotton goods.

The Lower and Upper Clayville Mills worked in conjunction with each other. They had a capacity of 20 hp, operated 108 looms, and employed 75 workers. In 1916 they were condemned for the Scituate Reservoir.

F. H. ALLEN, Treas.   INCORPORATED, 1847   O. H. LAWTON, Supt.

FREIGHT
EXPRESS and
POST OFFICE
ADDRESS,
PROVIDENCE, R. I.

OFFICE OF

THE ASHLAND COMPANY

Manufacturers of

COTTON GOODS

TELEPHONE,
827-12 AND 1515

Ashland, R. I. _____ July 10th 1902 _____ 190

To The Honorable The Town Council of The Town Of

Scituate R. I.

Hon, Sirs;-

   The undersigned would respectfully represent that they

desire to examine the Bridge over the Canal in the Highway in

Ashland and if found to be in need of repairs to make such as are

necessary , in order to do this it may be necessary to close the

said Highway during the time , therefore we would respectfully

request that your Honorable body take such action as will result

in allowing us to legally accomplish the above object.

     Very respectfully,

      Ashland Co.
       F. H. Allen Tras

The Ashland Co. was incorporated in 1847 and was located where the Plainfield Pike crosses the Scituate Reservoir. The mill produced cotton goods and employed 60 workers. It was sold at auction for $500 and the tenement houses were retained for the reservoir construction workers.

The Harrisdale Mill was located near the south end of Peeptoad Pond and was built by Asahel and Albert Harris. It was a two-story stone mill and had 28 looms. It changed owners many times and burned in 1875.

Jackson Mill was located on the Pawtuxet River between Fiskeville and Hope. It was built by Charles Jackson in 1823 and had 120 broad looms and employed 50 workers. It, too, changed hands many times.

The North Scituate Cotton Mill was located in the village of N. Scituate, opposite the present Horseshoe Dam. It produced two million yards of print-cloth annually. It was sold at auction for $832 with the stipulation that it be removed immediately.

This tenement village for the workers of the N. Scituate Cotton Mill, featuring single-family homes each with its own yard, was built to attract the best workers possible. This was a great improvement over the crowded tenement conditions of some mill villages.

The Ponaganset Mill was located on the Ponaganset River near Clayville. The first cotton mill was built in 1826 and was destroyed by fire. The mill shown here was built in 1854.

The Ponaganset Mill manufactured 4,000 yards of print-cloth per day. It employed some 65 workers, two-thirds of whom were women. In 1830 the average male earned $4.50 per week, while women earned $2 per week and children earned $.69 per week.

The Ponaganset Mill had its own hydroelectric plant with a capacity of 60 hp which powered 127 looms to make cloth.

This picture shows a large section of pipe which fed water from the Barden Reservoir to the power house.

The Remington Mill was located in the village of Rockland. It was erected in 1831 by Thomas Remington and produced cotton goods. Like all the Scituate mills, it was sold at public auction after the machinery was removed.

The Remington Mill Pond was typical of the ponds at most mills in Scituate.

The original Richmond Mill was built in 1812 and was located on the Ponaganset River. The mill had several owners before being destroyed by fire in 1877. The property was then purchased by William E. Joslin, who built this mill complex.

The Richmond Mill had a power capacity of 60 hp and contained over five hundred braiding machines which made shoe and corset laces.

This Rockland Mill was erected in 1856 on the Westconnaug Branch of the Ponagansett River in the southwest part of Scituate.

The Rockland Mill Hydroelectric Plant was typical of the power plants used by the larger mills in Scituate. This plant had a capacity of 75 hp.

The original Red Mill, located just above the Rockland Mill, was built in 1815. It was destroyed by fire in 1840 and was soon rebuilt.

This picture of the second floor of the Red Mill shows some of the 60 looms used to manufacture cotton cloth.

The Shoddy Mill was located near the Ponaganset Mill on the Ponaganset River. The mill got its name from the reprocessed fibers, referred to as "shoddy," which were used in the manufacturing process.

The Shoddy Mill Tail Race was used to access water to the mill. When the water level is low in the reservoir, it is possible to see the foundation of this mill near Tunk Hill Road and Plainfield Pike.

Three

Businesses

The Richmond Store and Post Office, located in the village of Richmond, was owned by William E. Joslin, who also owned the Richmond Mill. This was typical of the general stores in the mill villages.

The Brayton Store/Hope Post Office was located on Main Street in Hope Village. From 1912 to 1944, Bertha M. Brayton operated the store and was also postmistress.

The E.L. Young Store was located on Route 116 in Hope. Mr. Young was a dealer in dry goods, groceries, hay, grain, boots, and shoes.

This store was built in the early 1900s and was located in the center of Clayville. Because of its location, Clayville became a center for trade, barter, and sales in this area. Note the trolley tracks of the Providence & Danielson Railway.

Traveling markets were a welcome and familiar sight in Scituate. They traveled many miles on the outlying roads to accommodate the farmers.

3 Pr Shoes   *3 6*

Delivered to Clara Adams as per order

The Rockland Store and Post Office was located in the village of Rockland. As noted on the letterhead, the store sold a great variety of goods.

Rockland Village was one of the larger mill villages and had two barbershops.

The Whipple Hotel served as a wayside stop for stagecoaches in the 1800s. It also housed a barbershop, bank, and pool parlor. It was located in the village of North Scituate where the St. Joseph Church now stands.

The Battey Hotel/Baltimore House was located on Plainfield Pike in South Scituate. The taverns were a meeting place for social and political activities. It is said that Scituate had as many as 14 taverns in the 1800s.

Everett B. Dexter.

—DEALER IN—
Apples, Cider, Vinegar, Turned Posts, Etc,

TELEPHONE 2-L-6 SCITUATE.

North Scituate, R. I., Dec. 28, 1909.

Town of Scituate

To E B Dexter Dr

For shovelling snow

1 yoke oxen—1 man 10 hours — 4.00

3 men 10 hours — 4.50

$ 8.50

In 1882 Everett B. Dexter began to purchase property on both sides of Danielson Pike and Dexter Road about 2 miles west of N. Scituate village. After planting a prosperous apple orchard, he built a cider mill in 1902 and produced 1,000 barrels of cider vinegar a year. In 1913 he added a cooper shop and employed 12 men to construct barrels. By 1918 over 5,000 bushels of apples were harvested a year.

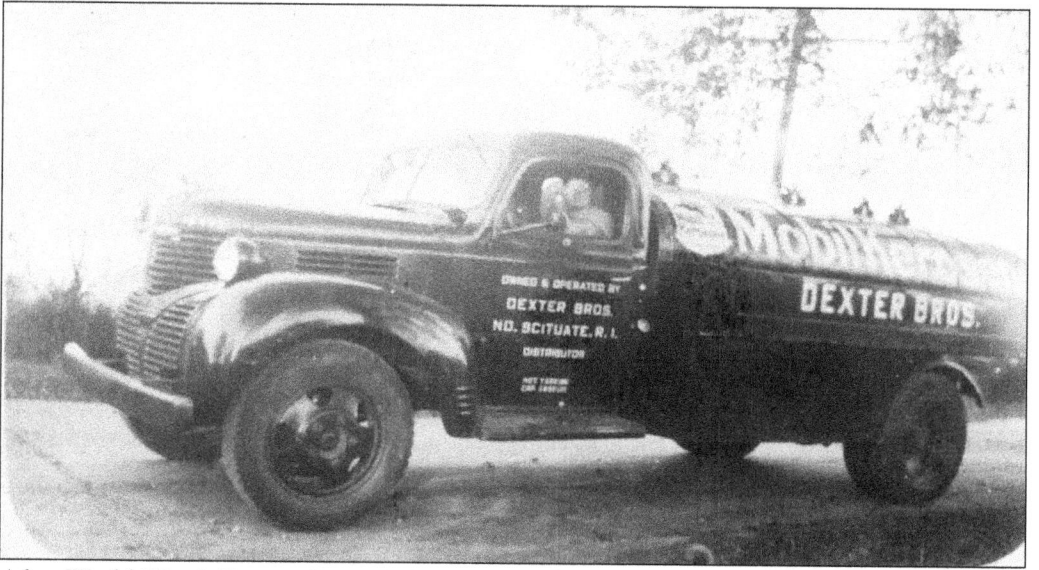

After World War I, Everett Dexter's Sons established Dexter Bros. and sold lumber, building supplies, and shavings. They later began delivering coal, firewood, and kerosene. Finally, fuel oil became their major business.

The Glenford Market was one of the smaller markets in N. Scituate village. It was located just west of the Horseshoe Dam.

The Hughesdale Ice Co. was located on Hartford Pike on the south shore of Moswansicut Lake. This large icehouse provided many carloads of ice which were transported to Providence by the Providence & Danielson Railway.

This icehouse was owned by Louis Hohler and had a capacity of 2,000 tons of ice. It was located near the Hughesdale Ice Co. These icehouses were insulated with sawdust and the ice lasted well through the summer. Ice was delivered daily to homes and businesses by Mr. Hohler right into the 1930s.

The South Scituate General Store and Post Office was located in Richmond Village. Leather-bound account books were a familiar sight in all the general stores. A typical entry might read: 1 lb. coffee .17, 1 pr. shoes $1.50, 1 yd. ribbon .04.

Before the days of automobiles, good roads, and supermarkets, these grocery wagons were a familiar sight. The routes of these traveling markets, which delivered a variety of goods and staples, extended for miles.

There were many family-owned apple orchards in Scituate in the early days. In the spring, the beautiful apple blossoms can still be seen on the remnants of the old orchards as well as on the orchards that remain in business today.

The W.H. Bowen Blacksmith Shop, located near the Horseshoe Dam in N. Scituate, was one of many blacksmith shops in the early days of horses and wagons. After it was condemned for the reservoir, W.H.'s son, Charles Bowen, continued to operate the business in the center of N. Scituate village until the 1950s.

One of the earliest garages in N. Scituate was Edwards Garage, located at the foot of Pine Hill Road. It changed hands many times and is still operating on the site as a garage.

The Scituate Insurance Agency was a familiar business in the village of North Scituate. It was owned by Sam S. Tourtellot, who was the town treasurer in Scituate for more than 50 years. Mr. Tourtellot erected the notable clock which has become a Scituate landmark.

Four

Transportation

Early transportation for schoolchildren was by horse and wagon. Schoolteachers often picked up the children on their way to school.

Transporting the cotton goods from the mills was done by horse and wagon in the 1800s. This picture shows the finished cotton goods leaving the Ponaganset Mill.

At the turn of the century, many women had their own horse-drawn buggies.

The Providence & Danielson Railway was extended to Scituate in the early 1900s. The trolley cars provided the first public means of transporting goods and people between Scituate and Providence.

49

The Providence & Danielson Railway Power House was located in Rockland Village. This power house provided the energy needed to send the cars on to Foster and Danielson. The cars were stored overnight and repaired, if necessary, at the Rockland Car Barn.

The Providence & Danielson Railway provided a means for the people of Scituate to travel between the villages for work and pleasure. The fare to travel from Providence to North Scituate was 20¢; to Clayville it was 35¢; and to Danielson it was 65¢.

The railway ran in all kinds of weather. In the winter the lack of sufficient power to plow the tracks after a blizzard caused service to be suspended until the cars could be dug out by hand.

Prominent mill owners were often seen being driven about by their chauffeurs, tending their stores and mills.

Land surveyors and their automobiles were a common sight during the condemnation of land for the reservoir.

Before the Town of Scituate owned large trucks, heavy snow was removed by men and boys shoveling by hand.

The roads were plowed by horses in the early days. As late as 1950, some lanes and driveways were still being plowed by Charlie Bowen and his horses, while the children enjoyed a ride.

NOTICE !

NO PERSON SHALL PLACE OR DEPOSIT STONES OR OTHER MATERIALS UPON ANY HIGHWAY IN THE TOWN OR ALONGSIDE THEREOF, SO AS TO OBSTRUCT OR INCOMMODE THE SAME, OR INTERFERE WITH THE REPAIRING OF THE SAME.

No Stones or other Materials shall be Placed or Deposited upon any Highway in the Town or alongside thereof, without the Approval of the District Highway Surveyor.

BY ORDER OF THE TOWN COUNCIL OF THE TOWN OF SCITUATE.

The Scituate Highway Department bought this road scrapper, which was used to level the dirt roads. It is still in use today.

The North Scituate Fire Department purchased its first new firetruck in July 1929. The truck was a Maxim with a 500-gallon water tank.

This 1920 tow truck was owned by Byron W. Page who operated the North Scituate Garage. The garage was located west of the Horseshoe Dam and was condemned for the reservoir.

These people were out for a pleasure ride in one of the early automobiles. Note the Providence & Danielson Railway tracks on the road going into Clayville Village.

The Spencer brothers had their own transportation, their wagon. They earned the money to buy this wagon by selling Larkin products to their neighbors. This picture was taken at their home on Silk Lane in North Scituate.

Five

Entertainment

This is the 1980 Armistice Day commemoration at the Old Congregational Church in North Scituate. This parade has been enjoyed by old and young alike for many years.

Bands were a popular pastime for men in the early days. The Glenford Band (above) is pictured in front of the Old Congregational Church. The bands played at local fairs, minstrels, parades, and other events. The Rockland Band (below) is shown at an event outside of Scituate.

The men often went snake hunting and fox hunting for recreation. The snake hunters would compete to see who could catch the longest snake, as snakes were in great abundance in this area. The fox hunters would congregate at the Town House on Trimtown Road, North Scituate, to begin their hunts.

After the Civil War, the Grand Army of the Republic Hall was built in the village of Rockland. Many social events were held in this hall to raise funds to decorate the graves of their fallen comrades.

FIRST GRAND SOCIAL.

Mr. *Charles W Olney*

Your company with ladies is cordially invited to attend a Social in

G. A. R. HALL, ROCKLAND,

Thanksgiving Eve, November 27, 1895.

HELD BY THE SOCIAL COMMITTEE OF

COM. PERRY COUNCIL, NO. 10, O. U. A. M.

WILLIAM KING'S ORCHESTRA.

TICKETS, $1.00 PER COUPLE, INCLUDING DANCING AND SUPPER.

Present this Card

Even though Harry Joslin knew the reservoir was coming, he built this beautiful dance pavilion in the village of Richmond. Weekly dances were held at the Richmond Casino and people came from far and wide to enjoy the dancing.

Keeney's Hall was located in Rockland and was built by Dwight Keeney. This was a popular spot for moving pictures, dancing, and entertainment.

The Grange Hall, located at Cleaner Chapel Road and Hartford Pike, was built in the late 1800s by the Wayside Gleaners. The N. Scituate Grange was organized in 1907 by local farmers to serve the agricultural interests of the area. The Grange took over the building in 1931. It is now the headquarters for the Scituate Preservation Society.

Local fairs were a yearly event that the people looked forward to. There were several locations for fairgrounds in Scituate; the larger one shown here was on Danielson Pike on the east side of Spring Brook Road.

32—OCT 7— 1913— N. SCITUATE FAIR—

The Fiskeville Fair was begun by the Ladies Bible Class of the Fiskeville Tabernacle Baptist Church to raise money. The gaily decorated booths and delicious food attracted many people who arrived by horse-drawn buggies.

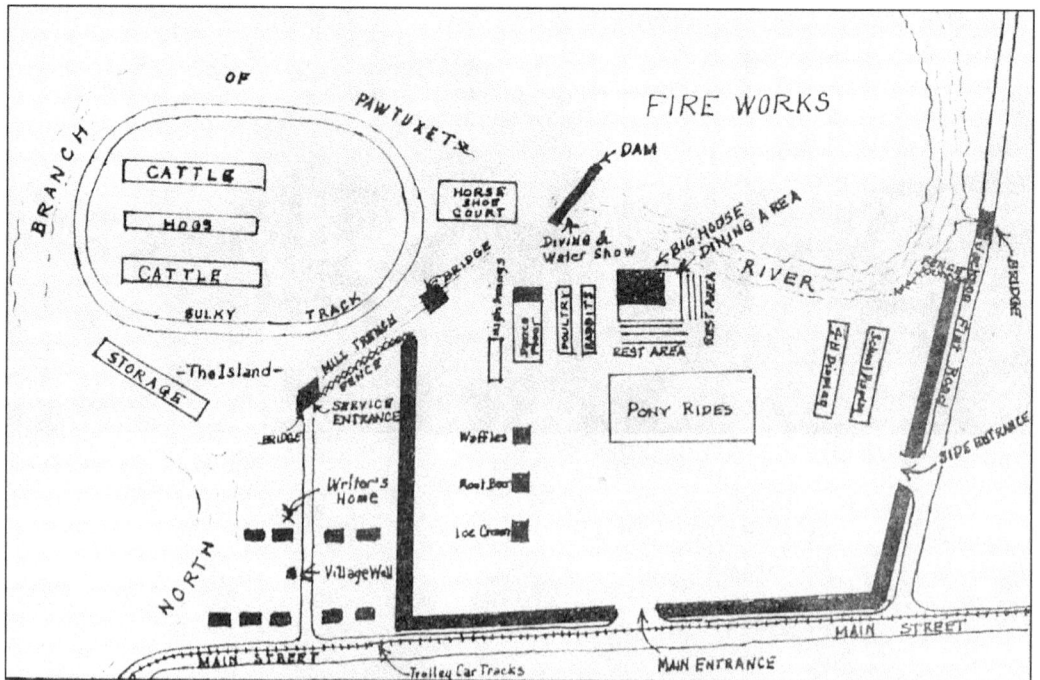

Memorial Day parades have traveled through Main Street in N. Scituate for many years and are still a popular event. This 1959 picture shows the Scituate Police Department, led by Chief Jack Crowley, leading the parade.

After laying the wreath at the Civil War monument, the parades always ended up at the Old Congregational Church.

For many years, the N. Scituate Fire Department #1 held a carnival at Berkanders Field, located opposite the Old Congregational Church. The purpose of this event was to raise money to purchase the trucks and equipment needed.

The volunteer firemen and their families constructed the booths and ran the concessions for the games and food. The whole town looked forward to the carnival with great anticipation. The children especially liked the turtle races.

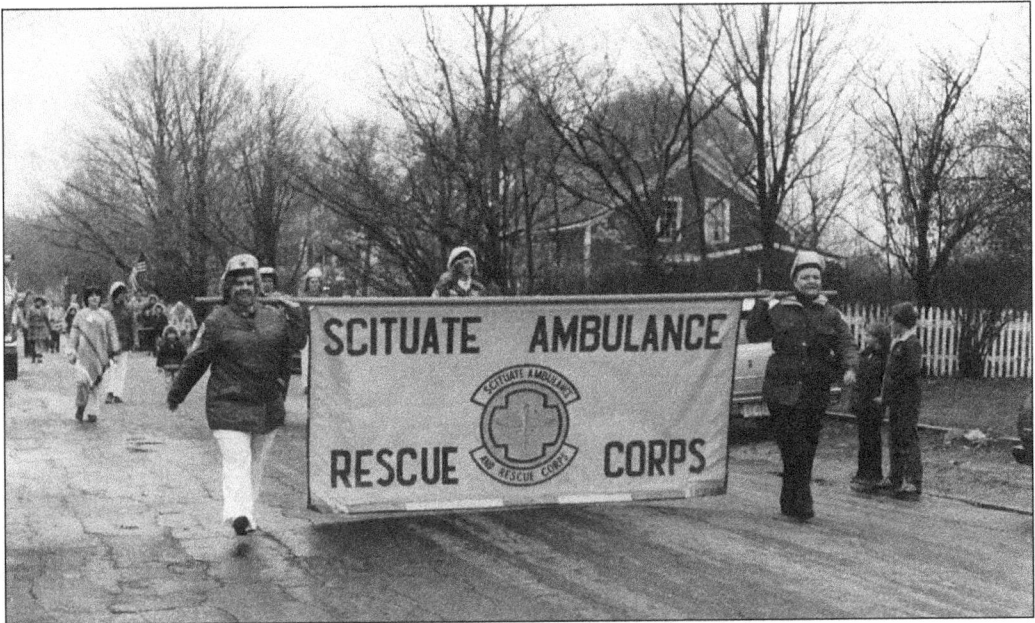

The Scituate Ambulance & Rescue Corps was established in 1953 by a group of dedicated volunteers led by Byron F. Hopkins and Thomas A. Bowers. The corps purchased its first ambulance, a second-hand Cadillac, for $2,000. The corps' volunteers continue to raise funds to purchase new equipment and train local EMTS. The corps' motto is: "We serve our God by serving our fellow man."

The Scituate Spartan cheerleaders lead the Scituate Jr.-Sr. High School Band. The band plays for parades, concerts, and other events.

The Scituate Art Festival was started in 1968 to raise funds to restore the Old Congregational Church, which was built in 1831 by the Smithville Society. From a beginning of a few artists, the art festival has grown to attract many artisans and craftsmen. Today it attracts more than 100,000 people every Columbus Day weekend.

HOME OF THE "FAMOUS APPLES THAT YOU CAN EAT IN THE DARK"

RESTAURANT

HIGHLAND ORCHARDS

HIGHLAND QUEEN

HIGHLAND & CIDER RIVER STEAM RAILROAD

The Highland Orchard Amusement Area was located on Hartford Pike on the site of Highland Orchards. It featured the Highland & Cider River Steam Railroad and the Highland Queen River Boat. Although there is no evidence of the train or the man-made pond today, this was a popular spot in the 1960s for family entertainment.

Six

Lost Villages

This picture of Richmond Village was typical of the mill villages condemned for the construction of the Scituate Reservoir.

The catastrophic impact of the loss of homes and property for the Scituate Reservoir is shown in this picture of the people selling their furniture, farm equipment, etc., at an auction. These auctions were a common sight in the Lost Villages of Scituate.

The condemnation of property was met with great resistance by many people. This woman held a gun at the condemnation men as she tried to protect the home that had been in her family for generations.

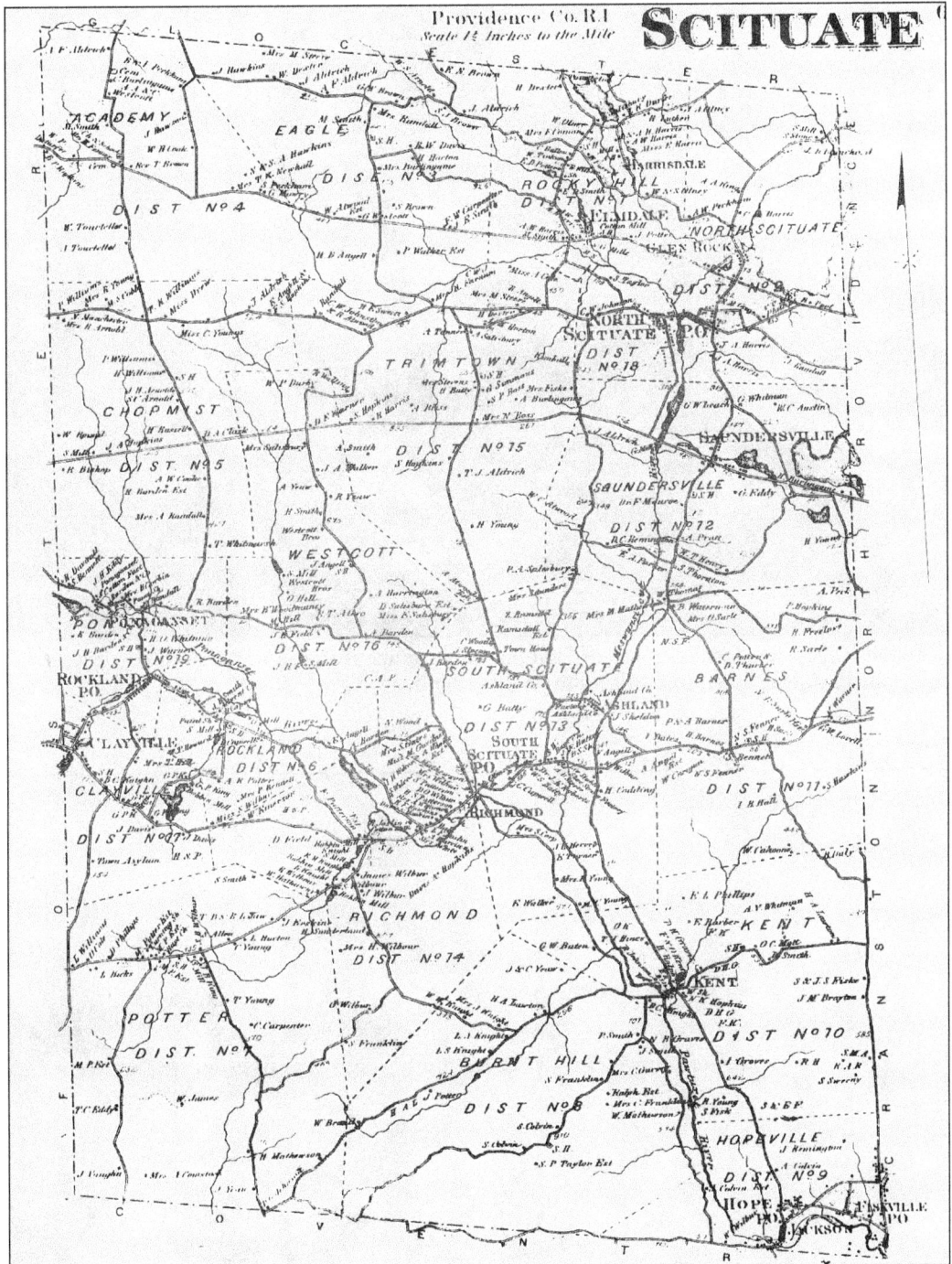

This 1870 Scituate map by D.G. Beers & Co. shows the Lost Villages and the 19 school districts.

ASHLAND VILLAGE — ABOUT 1910

Ashland Village was located south of Plainfield Pike at about the center of Scituate. It was said to be one of the prettiest mill villages in Rhode Island.

The village of Ashland was about 200 acres in size and was a flourishing manufacturing community. The City of Providence purchased the entire village for $200,000 in 1916.

72

The Union Church in Ashland Village was said to have been one of the prettiest churches in Scituate. It was built by the Ashland Co. about 1856 and was open to all denominations.

This building was the Ashland Store and Post Office. It had meeting rooms on the second floor.

Ashland Falls was located near the Ashland Mill, which was owned by Ferdinand Allen. His home, pictured below, was located on Village Street in Ashland.

The village of Clayville was once a thriving mill village located along the western border with Foster. It was settled in 1826 by Josiah Whitaker, who operated a factory and store there. These pictures depict the mill houses and Main Street in Clayville.

This picture of the Clayville Mill Pond, with the village of Clayville in the background, shows how beautiful the village was in the early 1900s.

The Upper & Lower Clayville Mills were powered by the hydroelectric plant, which got water from the mill pond. The foundation of this plant can still be seen off the main road.

The Westconnaug Reservoir is located on the Foster/Scituate line in Clayville. In the early 1900s many summer camps were located along its shores.

Clayville's mills were powered by water from the Westconnaug Reservoir and the Clayville Mill Pond. Such waterfalls as seen here were a common sight in many of the mill villages.

Old Bank Village
No. Scituate, R.I.

Elmdale Village, sometimes known as "Old Bank," was located at Hartford Pike and Elmdale Road. The first chartered bank in Scituate was located here in the early 1800s.

The Rocky Hill School, District 7, was located on the east side of Elmdale Road at the intersection of Rocky Hill Road.

This homestead, owned by Ansel Harris, was located on Peeptoad Road. Harrisdale was named for the Harris family, who established a mill there. Its ruins can still be seen off of Peeptoad Road.

PEEPTOAD GATE HOUSE.
NOV 4. 1915. J. R. HESS.

The Peeptoad Gate House was located on the outlet of Peeptoad Pond. Remnants of the raceway can still be seen today.

Kent Village was located where the Gainer Dam is today and was one of the smaller villages. The Kent Corners (or Four Corners) was on the road leading from Hope to South Scituate.

Kent Village consisted of the mill, church, school, and post office pictured above.

The Kent School, District 10, was built about 1845 and was a one-room schoolhouse. About 30 students were enrolled for 8.5 months and were taught by Mr. Angell.

The Christian Union Church was located at Kent Corners. It was organized in 1877 with Rev. Daniel Knight as its pastor.

The Knight family settled in the Kent area in 1708. The "Old Home" was owned by Lyman A. Knight and was built in the 1800s. Four generations of Knights were living here when the land was condemned for the reservoir.

The Tunk Hill Farm, sometimes known as the "Home of 7 Brothers and 7 Sisters," was owned by William W. Knight, brother of Lyman A. Knight. The Knights owned over 1,000 acres on Tunk Hill Road. Four Knight family cemeteries are still located on City of Providence property today.

The Glenford School, District 18, was located on the south side of Danielson Pike just west of North Scituate. It was a one-room structure with about 30 pupils enrolled.

The William Bowen Blacksmith Shop was located where the Horseshoe Dam is today on the north side of Danielson Pike. The land in the background was known as the "marshes."

This Quaker meetinghouse was located on the north side of Hartford Pike near the intersection of Routes 101 and 116. It was built in 1812 and was sold at auction in 1910 due to declining membership. For a century this little building was a well-known landmark in North Scituate.

This Pentecostal church was located on the west side of Silk Lane in North Scituate at the curve where the west entrance to the Smithville Cemetery is located.

This beautiful home was owned by William Bowen and was located in North Scituate on the west side of West Greenville Road near the junction of Routes 101 and 116. It was one of the many stately homes condemned for the reservoir.

Seaman's Grocery Market was located on the north side of Danielson Pike just west of the Horseshoe Dam at Card's Corners. This was where the Providence & Danielson Railway turned south to the mill villages.

Ponaganset Village was located near the western border of Foster/Scituate on the present Ponaganset Road. The village was originally known as Barden's Mill and then Bettyville after John Barden's wife. After the new mill was built there, it became known as Ponaganset. These mill houses were home to some of the 65 workers at the Ponaganset Mill.

Ponaganset School, District 19, was located on the west side of Ponaganset Road. This was a two-room school and was one of the 19 school districts in the early 1900s in Scituate.

The assembly hall and tenement house shown here were located in Ponaganset Village.

Richmond Village was located south of Ashland and was the original center of activity in Scituate. In the 1800s it was one of the busiest mill villages as it had many mills located there over a period of almost 100 years.

Richmond School was located on the south side of Plainfield Pike in District 14. It was built in 1849 and had an average enrollment of 25 pupils.

The first Trinity Church was built in Richmond Village in 1864. This beautiful church was taken by the City of Providence for the reservoir. In 1950 a new Trinity Church was built on land owned by the City of Providence on Danielson Pike, North Scituate.

Rockland Village was located in the western part of Scituate bordering on the north branch of the Pawtuxet River. This typical mill village had three well-known mills—the Rockland Mill, the Remington Mill, and the Red Mill. It also had several small mills and shops, stores,

churches, a school, post office, etc. The Joslin Manufacturing Co. bought the mills, water rights, and mill houses in 1901.

The Rockland School, District 6, was located in the village of Rockland on the south side of the present Tunk Hill Road. This one-room schoolhouse was built in 1823 and had an average attendance of 24 students.

The Rockland Christian Church was one of the six churches lost because of the reservoir. The church society was paid $2,500 for the property and was given free rent for five years with the option to remove the building if they wanted to.

Rockland was a busy mill village with many small businesses. These are two of the stores that were located there.

The village of Saundersville was located south of North Scituate off of Route 116. It was the site of three mills, a school, and about 25 homes.

The Saundersville School in District 12 was located on the west side of the present Route 116. This one-room school had an average attendance of 20 pupils.

One of the farms located in Saundersville was this Searle family farm, located on what is now the William Henry Road. The buildings were taken in 1920 by the City of Providence for the watershed.

After going through the village of North Scituate, the Providence & Danielson Railway turned south to Saundersville. The trolley stopped at Parkers Crossing, located at Parkers Grove, where school and church picnics were held.

South Scituate was located north of Richmond. These two villages were often confused with each other. The South Scituate School, in District 13, was located at the intersection of Battey Meeting House Road and Plainfield Pike.

The South Scituate Six Principle Baptist Church, also known as the Battey Meeting House, was located next to the school. This picture shows the interior of the Battey Meeting House about 1897.

The Shaffer House, formerly the South Scituate Post Office, was established in 1825. When the building was condemned, it was used as the headquarters for the Providence Water Supply Board's operations.

Town Clerks Office   Scituate, R.I.

This was the first official building for the town clerk. Prior to 1883 the clerk's offices were usually in the home of the clerk. After the condemnation of the building in 1921, it was voted to move the office to its present site in North Scituate.

One of the many homes taken for the reservoir was this large home, Forest View, owned by the Esleeck family. It was located on the north side of Plainfield Pike near the little village of Wilbur Hollow. This picture of the Esleeck kitchen was typical of the 1900s. Note the hand pump for water.

There were over 12 rooms in the lovely Esleeck home. One of the two parlors and one of the five bedrooms are pictured here.

Wilbur Hollow

Scituate. R.I.

Wilbur Hollow was one of the smaller lost villages in Scituate. It was located south of the present Plainfield Pike. The white building in the center of the picture became the Providence Real Estate Office when the property was condemned. Note on the lower picture that when the reservoir was filled, Wilbur Hollow was under 80 feet of water, as indicated by the dotted line.

Seven

The Scituate Reservoir

WATERSHED

A History of the Scituate Reservoir

Wendy Ketchum

This picture shows one of the many small cemeteries that had to be moved when the property in Scituate was condemned for the reservoir. The removal of the bodies brought great sadness to the families whose ancestors had been in the cemeteries for many years.

The New Rockland Cemetery, where the graves were moved to, is located in Clayville. This is the long winding road into the cemetery as it was being prepared. Today it is also known as Historical Cemetery #50.

The construction of the New Rockland Cemetery was considered to be a model example of how this type of project should be done. It was a monumental effort and was done with excellent documentation by local officials and the City of Providence.

Upon completion of this project, 1,485 graves had been removed from the reservoir site and 1,080 graves were relocated to the New Rockland Cemetery. Some burial grounds in the watershed area which were above the high water line were not moved.

The Winston Construction Camp was built to house the reservoir construction workers. Built on the Fiske Farm near Kent Village, just north of Hope, it seemed as though a whole new village appeared overnight. The workers came from other states and other countries and had to board with local farmers until the camp was completed.

At first the Winston Camp was small, consisting of three four-man bunk houses and a mess house. Later five more bunk houses were added along with a garage, stable, hospital, and an administration office. The camp was called "Shack Town" and "Mushroom Town." It was enclosed by a wire fence and had a three-man police force.

The construction of the Scituate Reservoir was one of the largest engineering projects in the state of Rhode Island. When the surveying began in 1913, Kent Village was one of the first areas to be condemned. These pictures show work in progress at Kent.

105

The first construction contract was awarded in 1917. After the completion of the reservoir, the following properties had been condemned and demolished or moved to other areas: 1,195 buildings, 375 dwellings, 6 cotton mills, 6 churches, 7 schools, 10 general stores, post offices, taverns, blacksmith shops, many smaller shops, the Providence & Danielson Railway, and about 30 large dairy farms.

These pictures show the immense size of the many tunnels that had to be excavated for the water pipe system necessary for the reservoir project. The sound of blasting for these tunnels became common once construction began.

A contract was made with Livingston Construction to pull out and remove the thousands of trees and stumps along the shore line of the future reservoir. The clearing of the trees began in the winter of 1923.

The Scituate Reservoir is shown here on December 17, 1925. The village of Richmond can be seen in this photograph, which was taken looking southerly from the canal upstream from the Richmond Mill. The ruins are the mill foundations; the water surface being 49 feet below the final flow line of the reservoir. Note the burning brush in the background.

The reservoir project disrupted the road system in Scituate, requiring the construction of 26.4 miles of new roads and the abandonment of about 32 miles of former roads. Several main highways, such as Plainfield Pike and Central Pike, had to be rerouted.

The McGovern Construction Co. was awarded the contract to build the Ashland Causeway on Plainfield Pike. Many local men were hired for the project. The construction of the causeway had to be stopped during World War I.

Looking west across the Scituate Reservoir, the Ashland Causeway (completed in 1925) can be seen. The reservoir was filled with water when this photograph was taken.

The Barden Dam, located on the Ponaganset River near Clayville, was built in 1883 to hold the water that powered the Ponaganset Mill. In 1884 the Barden Reservoir Co. decided to raise the dam 5 feet higher, using stones taken from the ledge nearby.

The Barden Reservoir covered 260 acres and became an integral part of the Scituate Reservoir. Today it is one of the most beautiful sights in Scituate.

These pictures show the construction of the Horseshoe Dam, located on Danielson Pike just west of the village of North Scituate. This water-regulating dam is 15 feet high and holds 421 million gallons of water.

The construction of the Horseshoe Dam began in 1918 and cost about $50,000. It was built on a gravel foundation on land once known as the "marshes."

J.R.HESS DEC. 17, 1925 NO. 1184

These pictures show the spillway located at the west end of Gainer Dam on the south end of the Scituate Reservoir. It is a reinforced concrete triple-arch bridge and the spillway carries the overflow of water from the reservoir at the time of high water. The process of cutting through the massive ledge for the spillway construction was a long and tedious one. The picture shows water going over the spillway into the Pawtuxet River.

The construction of the Gainer Dam took thousands of hours of manpower and years to complete. The dam occupies the site of Kent Village. The earthen dam is 3,200 feet long and 640 feet wide at its base.

The Gainer Dam was the major dam of the Scituate Reservoir project. It was named for former Providence Mayor Joseph H. Gainer. The plaque was designed by Aristide Cianfarani and was cast in bronze by the Gorham Manufacturing Co. It was dedicated in October of 1949.

In 1924 a contract was awarded for the construction of the water purification plant located on Route 116 near Hope. This picture shows the foundation of the head house and influent control chamber. The 94-foot steel pipes were laid on top of the main drain and two 60-foot pipes were laid in the base of the dam to connect with the purification plant.

The present purification plant, a large 2-3 story building, is located on the site of the original plant. Water is carried from the reservoir to the plant and on to the city of Providence by gravity.

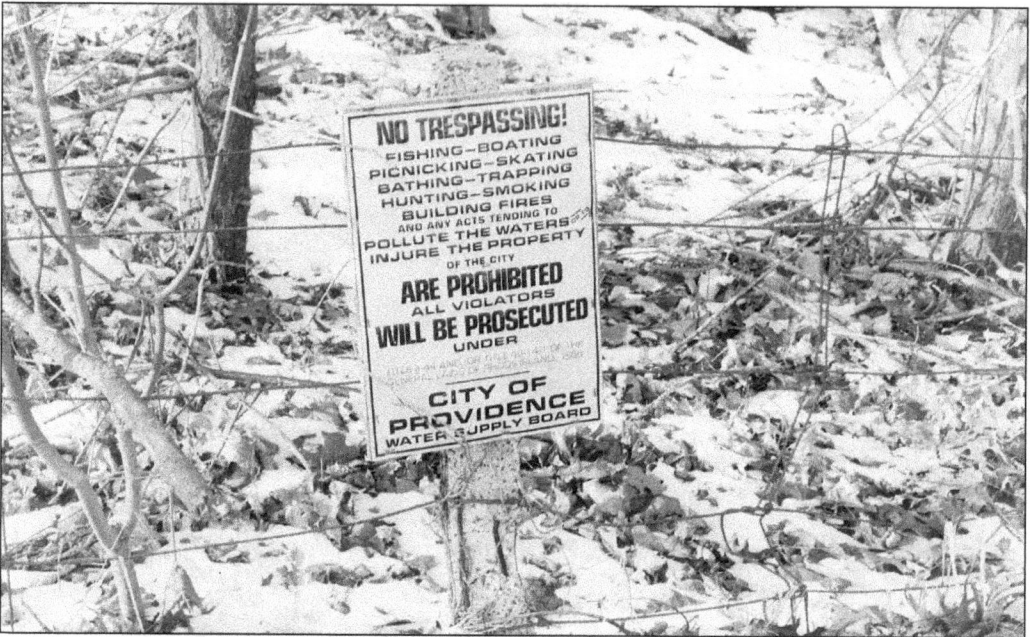

The NO TRESPASSING signs, which are posted along the miles of fencing surrounding the Scituate Reservoir, are a familiar sight today. Over seven million evergreen trees were planted to protect the watershed area.

Today we take for granted the serene beauty that makes Scituate a unique, rural town. However, we must not forget the great sacrifice that many Scituate families had to make to ensure the provision of clean water that the people of Rhode Island depend on today.

Eight

Scituate Today

As you travel south on Route 116 through the beautiful watershed area, you will see the water purification works of the Scituate Reservoir. To the left in this picture is the influent aerator, which removes carbon dioxide from raw water and eliminates disagreeable odor. The two large silo-like structures are used for bulk storage of chemicals. On the right is the Forestry and Maintenance Building. In addition to the Scituate Reservoir, five smaller reservoirs feed into the system, providing an average of over 50 million gallons of water a day to the purification plant.

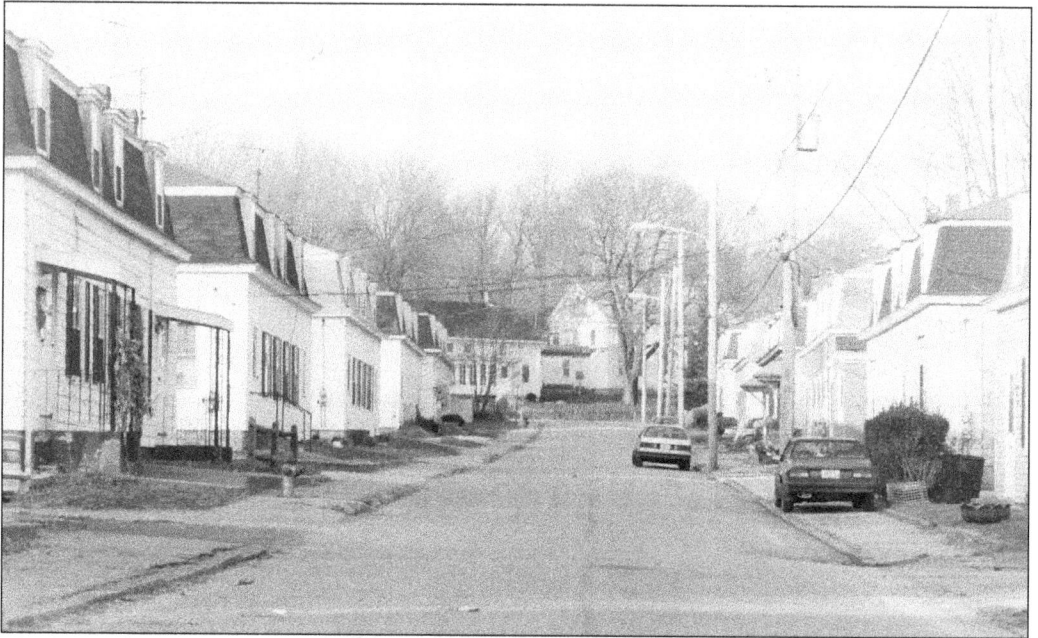

The village of Hope is located in the southeast corner of Scituate and has the only surviving mill in Scituate today. The Hope mill, mill houses, schools, stores, church, and other old buildings remain intact and are well preserved as remnants of its past history.

In 1927 formal plans began for the construction of the two-story brick Hope School. At that time, $110,000 was appropriated for the purchase of land, construction of the building, and the furnishings for the school. Because of the increase in the number of students in the Hope area, many additions and improvements have been made over the years.

The Hope Library is located across from Hope School on Route 116. It was opened in July 1966, after construction was completed at a cost of $44,000. There were 6,000 books in the collection at that time. A new addition was built in 1989 and was dedicated in June 1990.

This cannon was cast *c.* 1778 at the famous Hope Furnace. It is a rare 4.5-foot, cast-iron cannon with an 8.5-inch diameter and was mounted on granite in Barre, Vermont. Library fund-raisers told donors for the cannon project that Hope has a unique history because the Brown brothers established the Hope Furnace there. According to records, 13 cannons cast at the Hope Furnace were fired on Providence Bridge, July 4, 1776, celebrating the Declaration of Independence.

The building that houses the Scituate Police Department, located on Main Street in Hope, was the original Hope School. It was built in 1847, a three-room structure that was the largest school in Scituate, and was used as a community center for a short period before it was remodeled for the Scituate Police Station in 1933.

The Hope-Jackson Fire Co. was formed in 1925, and in 1930 the land for a new station was purchased from Mrs. R.G. Howland for $1,000. The school annex building on the property was converted into the present station. Chief Otis Luther, seen in the middle of the above picture, retired in 1958 after serving 33 years as chief. The Hope-Jackson Fire Co. continues as an active, volunteer fire company today.

The Hope Post Office is located on Main Street in Hope. It changed location several times along Main Street before being moved to its present location in 1946 at the corner of Main Street and Route 116. The building, built in the nineteenth century, was once known as the "Welcome Matteson" Hotel. It has been renovated many times.

The Fiskeville Tabernacle Baptist Church is located on Seven Mile Road near Hope. It was built in 1873 with solicited funds of $1,664.41. The Rev. Benjamin B. Cottrell was chosen as its first pastor.

121

The Potterville Fire Station held its first meeting in 1948. In 1979 they moved from the old station on Old Plainfield Pike to the new station on Tunk Hill Road. The Ladies Auxiliary played a very active role in the growth of this fire company, raising money at bean suppers, May breakfasts, and dances. There are four fire companies in Scituate today, all manned by volunteers who give many hours of service and who are greatly appreciated by the town citizens.

The old Potterville School, District 7, is located on the south side of Old Plainfield Pike. It was used as a community house in the 1940s. Restoration began in the 1990s by the Scituate Preservation Society to restore the one-room schoolhouse to its original likeness.

The Chopmist Fire Co. is located on Chopmist Hill Road on land donated by Percy Blackmore. At the first meeting in 1950 about 55 men enrolled in the company and 18 women enrolled in the Ladies Auxiliary. The original station was replaced by a new four-bay station behind the old one. Not only do the fire companies in Scituate respond to fire calls, they also spend many hours pumping out cellars, burning brush, etc.

The Clayville Post Office is located on Field Hill Road. It was built in 1846 and was the Clayville School, District 17, until 1933, when the new school was constructed. After the school closed, it was used as a community house until 1987, when it became the Clayville Post Office. It has recently been restored to reflect its historic background.

The Clayville Elementary School was built in 1933 and was one of the three schools built to replace the former one-room schools. Additions took place in 1956 and 1973.

This bell, from the Richmond Mill, is housed in a replica of the bell tower which was on the mill. It is located between the Old Congregational Church and the North Scituate Community House. In 1996 the Scituate Preservation Society sponsored the construction of the bell tower. The Joslin family donated the bell to depict Scituate's industrial past.

The North Scituate Community House is located on the west side of West Greenville Road in North Scituate. The front part of the building was the original two-room Academy School, District 2, built in 1825. In 1946 an addition doubled the size of the building. An original feature in the school was the miniature solar system, still imbedded in the ceiling. The community house is in constant use by the townspeople today.

The North Scituate Public Library is located on West Greenville Road. It was built in 1925 on land donated by Mrs. Henry W. Rice at a cost of $11,065. In 1984 an addition was built at a cost of $593,808. Today the library serves the public on the state-wide computer program, CLAN.

The Old Congregational Church is located on West Greenville Road. It was built in 1831 by the Smithville Society at a cost of $3,000. In 1940 the church was deeded to the town to be used for religious and historical purposes. In 1968 the Scituate Art Festival Committee was formed to raise funds for the restoration of the church. The beautiful church with its three-stage steeple remains Scituate's most famous landmark.

The Scituate Bandstand was constructed to commemorate the town's 250th birthday in 1981. This was a cooperative effort involving the Scituate Keeping Society, citizen volunteers, and the Public Works Department. The bandstand is the focal point of many local activities.

The Scituate Commons, an apartment complex, is located on Institute Lane in North Scituate. The original building was a three-story Greek Revival structure with two wings. It was designed by Russell Warren, a well-known Rhode Island architect. It was known as the Smithville Seminary when it was first built in 1839, the Lapham Institute in 1863, the Pentecostal Collegiate Institute in 1902, and the Watchman School & Camp in the 1920s—by which time the two wings had been destroyed by a series of fires. The present Scituate Commons was constructed in 1983.

The North Scituate Fire Department is located on Main Street in the village of North Scituate. In the early 1900s the first fire station was a garage located where the Horseshoe Dam was built. They were known as a "Rough and Ready Co." and their only equipment was an old hand-operated pump and wagon. After fire destroyed the garage, they moved to the old fire station across from the present station. This small building was home for the fire department from 1928 to 1951. The present station was built in 1951 on land condemned when the reservoir was built. The citizens of Scituate are very fortunate to have four active volunteer fire companies to assist at fire and rescue emergencies.

After the construction of the reservoir began, the town clerk's office was moved to its present location on Main Street in the village of North Scituate. This building houses the town offices and the Scituate School Department. We are proud of the continuing effort of the townspeople to preserve our town's heritage.